4

DEMON
STREAK

Text by JONNY ZUCKER
Art by STEVE SAMPSON

EDGE
FRANKLIN WATTS

LONDON•SYDNEY

DEMON STREAK

Max has bullied Ben since they were little kids
and he never misses a chance to make
Ben's life a misery...

First published in 2013 by
Franklin Watts
338 Euston Road
London NW1 3BH

Franklin Watts Australia
Level 17/207 Kent Street
Sydney, NSW 2000

Text © Jonny Zucker 2013
Illustrations © Franklin Watts 2013

The rights of Jonny Zucker to be
identified as the author and Steve Sampson
as the illustrator of this Work have
been asserted in accordance with the
Copyright, Designs and Patents Act, 1988.

A CIP catalogue record for this book
is available from the British Library.

ISBN: 978 1 4451 1799 7

Series Editors: Adrian Cole and Jackie Hamley
Series Advisors: Diana Bentley and Dee Reid
Series Designer: Peter Scoulding

A paperback original

1 3 5 7 9 10 8 6 4 2

Printed in China

Franklin Watts is a division of
Hachette Children's Books,
an Hachette UK company
www.hachette.co.uk

6

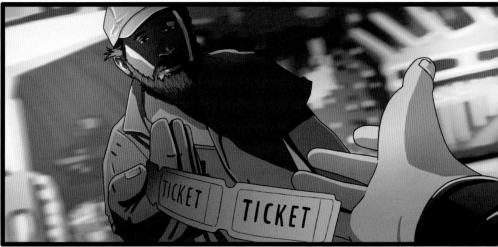

The next day.

Can we do something special today?

Sure, it's the weekend – what do you want to do?

Let's go to the leisure centre...

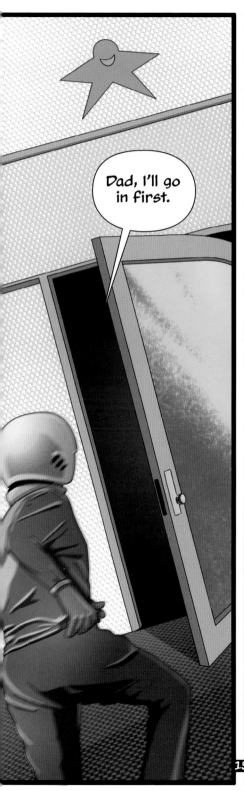

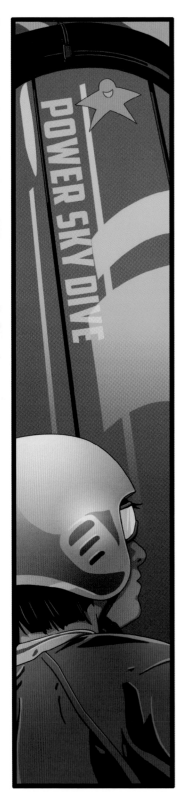

In Max's bedroom.

So, did you get Ben?

I thought you might be hungry—

I hate pepperoni on my pizza!

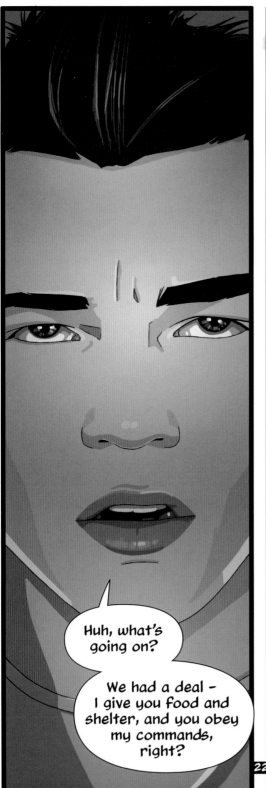

Wrong, you had a deal with *your* demon!

Huh, what's going on?

We had a deal – I give you food and shelter, and you obey my commands, right?

FOR TEACHERS

About

SLIP STREAM

Slipstream is a series of expertly levelled books designed for pupils who are struggling with reading. Its unique three-strand approach through fiction, graphic fiction and non-fiction gives pupils a rich reading experience that will accelerate their progress and close the reading gap.

At the heart of every Slipstream graphic fiction book is a great story. Easily accessible words and phrases ensure that pupils both decode and comprehend, and the high interest stories really engage older struggling readers.

Whether you're using Slipstream Level 2 for Guided Reading or as an independent read, here are some suggestions:

1. Make each reading session successful. Talk about the text or pictures before the pupil starts reading. Introduce any unfamiliar vocabulary.

2. Encourage the pupil to talk about the book using a range of open questions. For example, what would they do if they had a demon? Would they use their demon for good or bad?

3. Discuss the differences between reading fiction, graphic fiction and non-fiction. What do they prefer?

Slipstream Level 2 photocopiable **WORKBOOK**
ISBN: 978 1 4451 1797 3
available – download free sample worksheets from:
www.franklinwatts.co.uk

For guidance, SLIPSTREAM Level 2 – Demon Streak has been approximately measured to:

National Curriculum Level: 2b
Reading Age: 7.6–8.0
Book Band: Purple

ATOS: 2.0*
Guided Reading Level: I
Lexile® Measure (confirmed): 310L

*Please check actual Accelerated Reader™ book level and quiz availability at www.arbookfind.co.uk